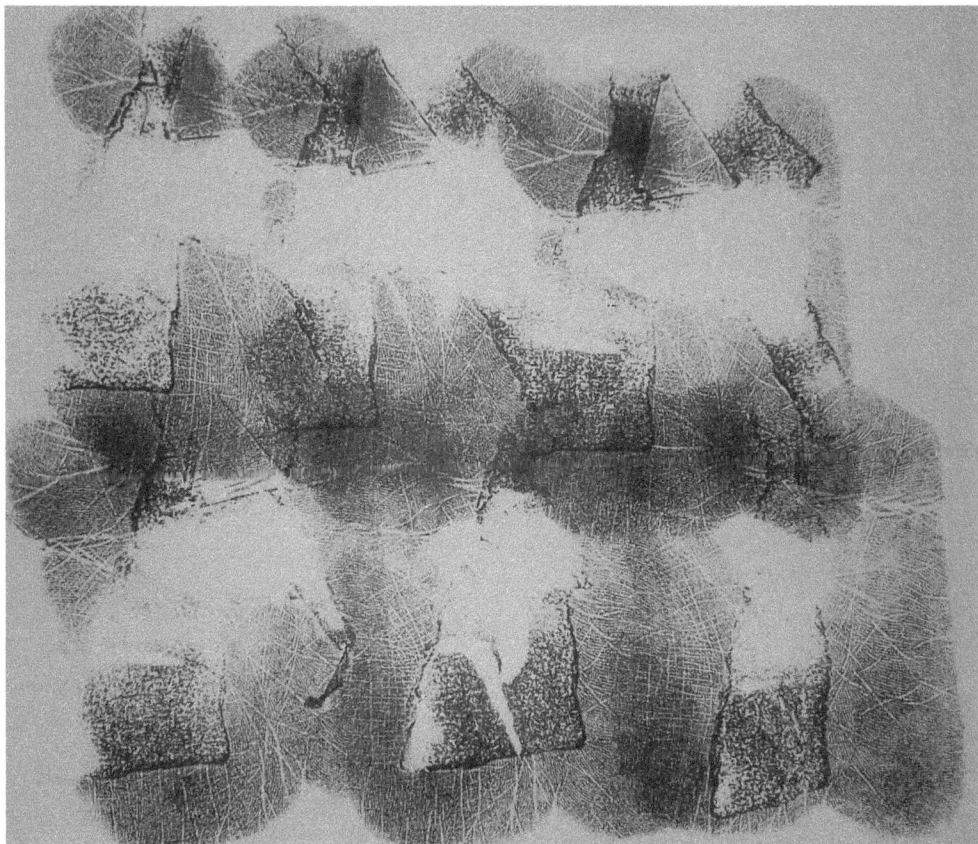

OH NO MY SELECTA by Richard Capener

YOU'VE GOT SO MANY MACHINES, RICHARD!

Ed. Dastidar & Kent

ISBN: 978-1-915079-99-2

The authors have asserted their right to be identified as the authors of this Work in accordance with the Copyright, Designs and Patents Act 1988

Cover design by Aaron Kent

Edited by Rishi Dastidar & Aaron Kent

Typeset by Aaron Kent

Page 1 interior illustration: 'OH NO MY SELECTA' by Richard Capener

Broken Sleep Books (2022)

Broken Sleep Books Ltd
Rhydwen,
Talgarreg,
SA44 4HB
Wales

Contents

You've got so many machines, Richard! an anthology of Aphex Twin poetry

Edited by Rishi Dastidar & Aaron Kent

Forewords

How do you explain a mystery? There has always been something suitably opaque to me about Aphex Twin, ever since I first came into contact with the idea of him, way back in the mists of the early 1990s. A friend had got hold of a copy of Warp's first *Artificial Intelligence* album, but in those days the myths were easier to get hold of than the music. There was – and is – something that remains pleasing about this; that he is generous enough to provide you with the space in which you can tell all and every kind of story.

    Should you explain a mystery? This opaque mythology is something that pervades a lot of the poems here, and I love the fact that none of our contributors have tried to attack this brief head on. Instead, they've been inspired by the sideways, the askew, the fables of him. That feels both pleasing, and right. You won't get to know Aphex Twin better through these poems, but you will be intrigued, all over again. And moved. That often gets forgotten, or lost: for all the electronics, the calculations, the futurity, the complexity of what he makes, he is actually the most emotional of musicians, and a reminder that brain and heart can – long to – get pulled at by the unexpected as much as the nostalgic familiar.

— Rishi Dastidar

I grew up in the shadow of Aphex Twin, a very faint shadow but it was there nonetheless. He had grown up in Redruth, Cornwall, and had gone to the same school as me many years prior. My dad would play various Aphex tracks around the house, but I didn't really click onto him until I discovered the song *Redruth School (Polygon Window)*. Once I found myself down the rabbit hole, I saw signs of him everywhere, from rumours he lived in a treehouse at the top of Lanner Hill, to rumours he drove a tank around town at night. None of this was true, but it didn't matter. Aphex was, and remains, an enigma, tank and all.

    That's what this anthology offers — absolutely no answers. This isn't intended to be a discovery of who Aphex is, nor necessarily what he means to our contributors, rather an attempt to introduce the mythos and aura of Richard D. James. This anthology aims to showcase, as Rishi writes in the above paragraphs, the 'brain and heart' of the music, and the soul of a man who may or may not exist as we know him.

— Aaron Kent

Well I know just how you feel

And now the new love
I know you love
will be there
even when I never find it
I know you love
will be there
even when I never find it
And now the new love
I know you love
will be there
even when I never find it
I know you love
will be there
even when I never find it
And now the new love
I know you love
will be there
even when I never find it
And

Whenever you can't sleep I play you Aphex Twin

In preparation for your birth I made a playlist
with the fraught care of a teenager curating a mixtape
for the only person
they'd ever love

Aisatsana [102]
Avril 14th
#3

Every night I listened, inhaling tranquil melody
imagined I could keep your heartbeat safe
beneath a veil of skin
within a liquid cave
while slow synth cocooned us both

Twenty hours deep
I laboured in the dark
warm waves breaking
over the ragged shore that I'd become

as languid piano mirrored each contraction
as ripples disturbed the surface of the pool
as soft chords spiralled into chaos

The next day, in a room
of brightest white
you were dragged from me, medicated slither
the only music an erratic bleep

98
126
75

it signified your heart was packing in
and made it clear
that a hypnotherapy playlist
        wouldn't cut it here

with metal clamped around your face
you screamed at silent air

So now
whenever you can't sleep
I play you Aphex Twin
in the hope that you recall the water
and the way
it should have been

On Alberto Balsam

yes, I've seen this place in my dreams. eternal song, why is it
so holy? when you have lost everything, a beautiful fall to sleep

gone cold, the memory is really the sound of growing up
too fast in the city. friendship as important as breath
broken in the dark from the mouth of the almighty herself

heard in an empty mall, in my dad's car

in the bright puddles, distant, we swam out
and the shampoo literally smelt like this

so clean, grey atmosphere but happy

haunted for years
this makes me actually feel something

like arriving late at night in your home airport
where the air is cool but familiar again. something
so specific and wordless, longing relief

like a hug from nobody at all. my fridge humming like nothing
even happened. I eat this song, keep hearing it

honestly in all my days

Your first iPod

2004. You at the height of your powers,
mine already on the wane.
You visiting in Mum and Dad's Mondeo,
me shotgun, your iPod classic in my lap,
lead trailing to the aux socket on the stereo.
We drive down dual carriageways
to Aphex Twin, *Come to Daddy*
volume up instead of talking.

I keep a picture of your iPod on my laptop screen
for seven years. Until academia spits
me out, partially digested.
The iPod's from the band you toured with,
a thanks for producing their album.
When were we last at a gig together?

Music makes me homesick for you.
Sitting in that Mondeo with you.
The speakers you positioned
in Mum and Dad's living room
for the ultimate listening experience.
You explaining twelve-part harmonies,
our partners exchanging glances beside us.
Big little brother, when this is all over,
I'll drive across the country to find you.
I'll bring the music of our youth.

Music Makers

we
are
those predisposed to smile widely at the
broad accusations of making   "electronic music
" what music is not electronic   ?   the makers
of animal hide drums and
ribcage osteophones were programmed by
Na+/K+-ATPase synaptic pulse just the same as we
kesson daleks in a shell of ambient tehcnohaze or aerosolized peyote are
just the same as ableton wielding windowlickers the
men in aurochs skull skull-caps inhaling campfire smoke incense the most analog dream
lurching forward millennia becoming prehistoric memories of
themselves the xtal balls flutter in your eye sockets you never remember your dream

Redruth School (Polygon window)

The tone is that of a butterfly
wearing a backpack, strapped
to its underbelly.

*(I figure it'd carry nectar,
right? Thats what butterflies
would carry in backpacks.)*

It's those seven trumpets signalling
the end of all things, blaring itself
across our faces.

*(it lives in the back of
my mind since I saw that 2011
Kevin Smith film, Red State.)*

Satanic chants like I don't even
know if that's true or if you're
lying about lying again.

*(lying as myth as a drum
machine for 5th period
geography.)*

I want to get a GCSE in you
but our school forgets you ever
existed, ever resisted.

*(The song has neither trumpets
nor chants but why let the truth
get in the way of story)*

Whenever I drive a tank around
my hometown, which is never,
I think of you in a treehouse.

wireless connection

what is this place ?
it smells like eggshells
the crack of the phone screen
bleeding light &
sound funnelled   into earphones
< all in tune >
the currents   of the sky
encased in wire
the soundtrack to
the morning's cigarette
broadcast from space
to my ears
< all connected >
tuning in and out
expanding smoke
clouds / fills the void
between skies
and clouds

entangling clouds

as the song
runs out of notes and
the last drum crackles
into birdsong silence
and some unseen magpie
fills his morning
with content
sitting crisp
against the sky
claw gripping the aerial
wobbling/warbling   more
with every caw against
this solar powered morning
this crack of dawn
light bleeding through the clouds

all eggshell white

all gently breaking apart

Dan Power

OPS WENT XANTHINE *(phonic boy on dope doped up to the max on vax mix)*

tiepawn paxwhip tinawn expath xaphex
weptthaw phatxi hepxi tapwhit exthaw
tanwith wipehew nihex newpath phatnix
pithpen netwith pixnet enthax awnpet
twinapt axhew thawpen thawpan phatwhip
phiawn extap xiapt wenhix weptxi
axwhet pitpith tinhex petwhit pithhewn
xhepni exphi nixwan piewax naphex
apthew winhex pintaw pintwin hipent
tinxi pawtap hapnet nexthap phinet
exwhit thawxi nixthaw weptax pawhex
pathwhen awnwit whexpi tinnext pixwept
tinpawn winphat whipwe aptphi wantpix
whetxi tanwex tenwax aptxi hiphex

On Spotify there's an official Aphex Twin playlist titled 'iTunes'

Deliciously, it's empty.
I've been here before, secreted in cables
of fungible meaning. You're out tonight
in the caustic biography of permaculture.
"We'll spend a portion of the money
on planting trees"
at the listening party on future planets
we'll plan fresh caresses, triple axis
on icicle triplicates, user sensoria, oratory
and into the blank.
So I dream holistic
eternal vice garden
with claims to marginal flower
and into the ache
auction all
close to the bleach tree, singing
infernal blip or lush
this sequencing technique
will help you realise

"You've got so many machines, Richard!" ▮▮▮▮▮ getting over Mötley CrÜe & Suicidal Tendencies ▮▮ he never got this dance ▮▮▮▮, my brother in the army. ▮▮▮▮▮▮ bought the vinyl of *'I Care Because You Do'* because ▮▮▮▮▮▮▮▮▮▮▮▮▮▮ bet he done it himself. ▮ played it ▮▮▮▮▮▮▮▮▮ in my room. ▮ just wanted to grow up ▮▮▮▮▮▮▮▮▮. *screeeeeeeeeeeeeeeeeeeeeee* ▮ came with a fold out poster of the painting on the front. ▮▮ evil massive, grinning face. ▮ didn't put it up. ▮▮▮▮▮▮▮▮▮▮▮▮▮▮▮▮▮▮▮▮▮▮▮▮▮▮▮▮. *Stop making that big face!!* ▮▮▮▮▮ this book called 'Iceberg Slim' ▮▮▮▮▮, ▮▮▮▮▮▮ nasty little ▮▮▮. ▮▮ beat the life half out of some girls, then run them a bath. ▮▮ in my head ▮▮ this connects with that. The punches ▮▮ the soft words. *screeeeeeeeeeeeeeeeeeeeeeeeeeeee* Ribs and knuckles cracking. Warm scented steam drifting ▮▮ *screeeeeeeeeeeeeeeeeeeeeeee* ▮▮ someone's voice breaking. ▮▮▮▮▮▮▮▮▮▮▮▮▮▮. *eeeeeeeeeeeeeeeeeeeee eeeeeeeeeeeeeeeeeeeeeeeeeee* ▮ gave all my old records away.

apoplex-perplex-complexities

bicarbonate frenetics; *the genesis?*
multi-generational, tape-to-tape
deck dubs, their foamy flumes of
playback hiss as rattly, miscued
mixtapes mis-struck in bonkerz
flanged brushstroke percussives
of amp-max gated smash o'snare -

metronomic melismatic wonk,
polychromatic sub-glottal alien
sprechgesang aligned to time
signatures noodled in varispeed;
in fraying flays o'dubsy drubbin'
vectored beatz. nu-alt clubbin'
zeroed in on decorous glitchin'

and adhoc, thereof, repeatings
as if spiked reportage to mux
a retro cha-cha stomp distort
to crunching churns irradiate;
to arcing, vaulting interference
compacting in a vice of abstruse
its apotheosis to gungey grunge -

maced in such displace, an aura;
billowed streaks astray in strobics,
we all, thrift of light limb, aflail in
apoplex-perplex-complexities.
Aphex *et al* in the cans, sofa-slothing
in Glaxo infused confuse of veiled
glissando drippage, arhythmic

mallow sonics of opaque,
oracular, aural twistesse;
irregular polygons transduced
to audible, to choriambic
vassals in vibrato sensoria,
splice-spruced micro-loops,
re-up sampled to peak infinities
flippering as fractals in mid-air…

rhubarb

i studied the angels of the night
i had wonderful dreams soundtracked by cornish waves
i had light printed onto paper
i collected blue rhubarb sprouting by the illogan park gates
i dropped acid & saw swans swimming on the moon
i jumped from the balcony, looking out at the beaches of xtal
i took a stone from the river & strung my shoes from the neon lights
your sister sang me soundless melodies, her selected ambient works
i began to lose my mind
you hit me with the sole of my shoe
i recovered

Dodecahedron

When I was bored, I'd take her for a drive.

It would be night time, clouds, rain 'n everything.
Cow parsley bustling, rabbits inventing myxomatosis,
no saxophone moon in sight.

I liked the darkness, the everyday nothings.
So did she.

She's not dead,
would be easier if she was dead (yeah, I said it),
she's just not around me anymore.

(9)

Computer Controlled Acoustic Instruments

Dummkopf broke a bucket
Trick shot ricochets
Punchcard dice dots shuffle
Dinky limbs of stick men

Angle grinding rusted
Stubborn rubber buttons
Raucous cherry picker
Cranks the forklift chorus

Tipping chicken, tapping corn
A long scrap timber marimba
Thinking in the dark to
Thickly markered barcodes

Your ball peen hammer pitting
Each wincing tinfoil inch
Sawdust skitters, scattering
Dings and intense dents

Smack the crusted ketchup sing
Cueballs mincing cymbals
Complex muffled impulse
Goes snapping off the pump clips

There's
a very fine line between being scared and

concerned. Since I don't like to say I'm
scared,
I say I'm concerned. But, you know what? I
really might be a little bit scared.
Yes?

Could
you tell me a bit about the mechanisms

on your bike? Well, it's a skycycle actually,
honey.
It's not a bike. A skycycle. There are only
two skycycles in the whole world and
I

have
them both. I had three, but the third

one is in the bottom of the Snake
River
Canyon. Are you one of those girls for whom
time stands still once a month? Are
you

one
of those girls for whom time stands still

once a month? Are you one of those
girls
For whom time stands still once a month? Are
you one of those girls for whom
time

stands
still once a month? Are you one of

those girls for whom time stands still once
a
month? Are you one of those girls for whom

time stands still once a month? Are
you

one
of those girls for whom time stands still

once a month? Are you one of those
girls
For whom time stands still once a month? [brand
name deleted] Why stop when the period
starts?

Are
you one of those girls for whom time

stands still once a month? Are you one
of
those girls for whom time stands still once a
month? Are you one of those girls
For

whom
time stands still once a month? Are you

one of those girls for whom time stands
still
once a month? Why stop when the period starts?
[brand name deleted] Why stop when the
period

starts?
Are you one of those girls for whom

time stands still once a month? Why stop
when
the period starts? Why stop when the period starts?
Why stop when the period starts? Why
stop

when
the period starts? Why stop when the period

starts? Why stop when the period starts? Why
stop
when the period starts? Why stop when the period
starts? Are you one of those girls
For

whom
time stands still once a month? Are you

one of those girls for whom time stands
still
once a month? Why stop when the period starts?
Oh get me another tie, Get me
another

shirt,
Get me another woolly, Evrrrryyydaaaaayyyy. Because have things

piling over me, have too many things, and we
having,
well my husband saying:"Ohhh". Oh get me another
tie, get me another shirt, get me
another

woolly,
Evrrrryyydaaaaayyyy. Because have things piling over me, Have

too many things, and we having, well my
husband
saying:"Ohhh". Oh get me another tie, get me
another shirt, get me another woolly, Evrrrryyydaaaaayyyy.
Slean

and
oh sometimes the way you read things the

way you see things hurts my heart I
fear
somehow they'll find the need To spit out my
name like a watermelon seed sometimes I
think

Milk Man

I wish   the milkman

3.5 mm stereo plug socket

A

B

rj

rj

rj

Stereo headphones

33 + 45 Ohms

AFx 100 Transformer

would   deliver   my milk

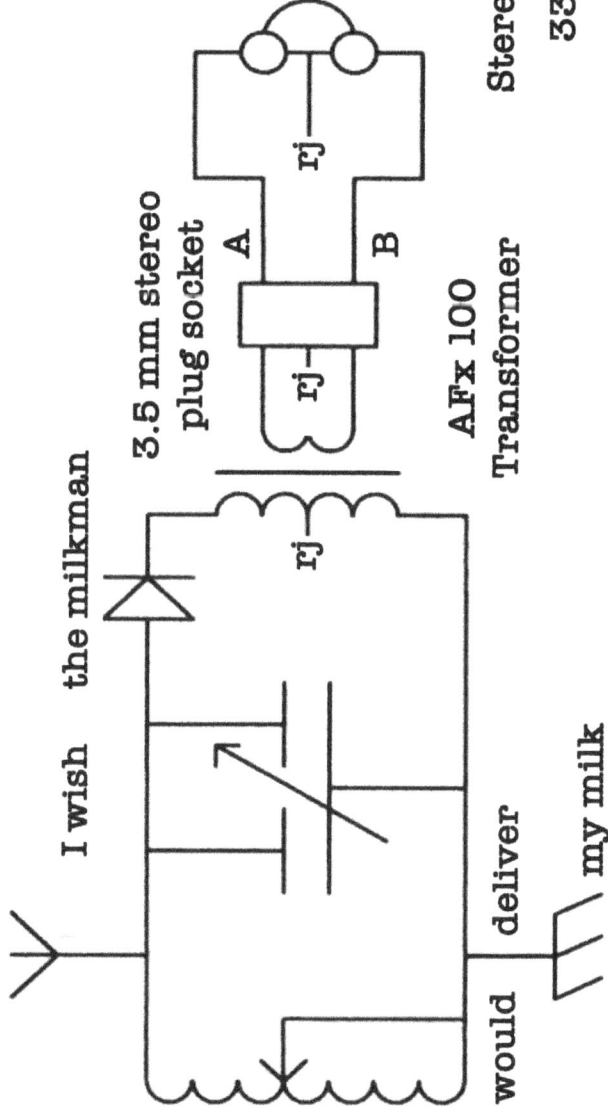

in the morning

Selected Ambient Words 85-21(∞)

(x)anadu;
(t)errarium

(a)bsolute;
(l)anguage

●

(tha)wing a
(tha)llophytic
(tha)tching-over
of (tha)notological
naph(tha)lene w/
(tha)nks –
(tha)t's all we're doing
    honest

●

the (pulse) of the synth lights the (width) of a word
the (pulse) of a word slights the (width) of the synth

●

we are born
we are zero
we are bathed in the wave
sine, sine, sine

we are warm
we are seven
the record is ready
sign, sign, sign

we are borne
we are twice seven
asleep on the motorway
sine, sine, sine

we are worn
we are five times seven
writing this poem
sign, sign, sign

(page is silo)
(age is polis)
all in time
except in this

sine, sine, sine
sine, sine, sine
whereof one cannot speak
sine, sine,

•

lyric-( )

•

oxide
formally (calx)
makes a poet (green)
with mineral envy

•

       (heliosphan)
it is sunshine – | who conjured sunshine
with a god in it! | with a god in it

•

       (music)

(we   are   the)   poets, (makers) of   mer
e   satellites   orbiting   solar   pianos
to   feel   as   the   critters we   are

•

(scho)ol day, e
(t)oo(t), o(k) –
h(ey), we love
the! (7th path)

•

at the centre
of the solar
system is a
synthesizer

& little we
the vast debris
listen close
(ptolemy)

•

(hed)   onism
(phel) tip-pen
(ym)   i here lol

•

(delphi)
say (um)
poets
be crumb

                e

•

the mulch
deepens
by this much

(act) upon (i)

reverie
reverie
how much?(um)

un10

a sestina for robot musicians

In al-Jazari's water-robot band,
designed 800 years ago, a weapon
bearer flanks a king. Adopted sky
is welcomed to the belly of the boat,
appearing as a transfer along the surface
of the water, sluicing beneath the music.

And the water is the very music
of it, churning life among the band
by way of cam-shafts, rolling cell-shaped surfaces
against pistons, plunging, playing. The weapon
and its king are still at the head of the boat.
Above the micro-scene: a tall sky.

Life-sized, amongst the reddening sky,
the chinking pulse and reeds of music
played by robot *qiya* from the boat
are clapped by drinking hands. A luminous band
of purple wine lines throats of guests like weapons
in sheaths, and centuries settle like snow on surfaces.

Fantailed papier-mache fish break surface
as clockwork fireworks chime like foil. The sky's
a red like bludgeoned liver, now, and weapon-
like arms make rings of hours. The maths of music
means that anytime is every time. The band,
a series of stark miniatures, clock the boat

through a forever of half-hours, boat
and band a fragile technology, until they resurface,
diskhats all prepared and mixed, to a sky
scored by millenia, a kind of contraband
of code designed inside a piano's music,
sounding now like weapons scraping weapons.

The crowd's a band of eyes. Screens are weapon-
ising facial recognition in the sky. Boats
claim the surface. Beneath, like shrapnel, music.

Days that don't exist

Out of the labyrinth jumps
the genesis of sound,
robotic humanity
in fancy dress.
Break it all apart,
every hidden message,
then pull back your top lip
and smile.

I left you asleep in the wood for a second,
dreaming of miners, mutations and tanks,
drowning in 3D constructions and hums,
disguised by decoding and deposit boxes.

Back from the coastline appears
a figure of folklore,
a fluctuating wave,
cloaked in resistance,
the elaborate chaos
of sonic isolation.
Now pull back your top lip
and smile.

He said Polynomial - C

whoforgetsall   unlearnseverything

Cigarette lighters   Cornish slurry
Modified amber decay   and menace.
Lorry driving   lucid dreaming
Tank on Teufelsberg satellite   and liminal submarines.
Distance   is   space.
A design   for   no one

whoforgetsall   unlearnseverything

That time   at Trezor
180 bpm   on the off chance
No   dance
45 gigs with a private dancer
shopping mall   plastic chairs
C- sandpaper   and   C- blender

whoforgetsall   unlearnseverything

Carry white   noise   Caress inmates
form   The   deranged
something about   an obsessive.
Desire   and desire to justify the lines.
Brave   a lid-less 101
Unlicenced   range   source unknown
A single cell   in a field   'A'   Sonic manipulator

whoforgetsall   unlearnseverything

To see   A different frequency
Potentiometer 100hz and below the abysmal
unequalised   and unmatched.
Other   than   a toilet cistern
it could   be transcendent.
A singularity   with polymorphic
        contours.
        Metaphrastic.
You told us   all along
C – an analogue C- bubble bath

whoforgetsall   unlearnseverything

Crowd Pleaser

Donkey Rhubarb & alex chopping lines / stefan says *i bet in this city somewhere we could find a man fucking a donkey* / *it's just a matter of money* i say / alex says *i wish i was a meteor* / stefan says *i'd hate to fuck a donkey* / i've been up for three days & a black cat darts across the ceiling / *too much fucking shit going on everywhere* i say / *my only ambition is to explode* says alex / stefan says *i might fuck a donkey if the whole room really wanted me to* / *rhubarb's fucking rank* I say / *if everyone was cheering me on chanting stefanstefanstefan i might do it* / *crowd pleaser* i say / *i'm a fucking planet* says alex / Avril 14th next & the mood shifts.

Ambient Works 02-03

He put it on my tongue
Melty nerve meat

Ambient fall
Clingfilm coffin

Love and love
The sick surprise
In the egg

Boy with light
Carried me to Paris
Clingfilm chrysalis

Fell from his grasp
Split my head
Off it all

One me still there
Clingfilm larynx

One me still there
In the ambient fall

Nothing is Ever Repeated (Sonnet 82454201)

Tape decks hissing, flummoxed in the grass
The boomerang returns, steeped in data.
Turning to love / when the frame rate drops
we could always go outside? Dreaming headshots.
Let's talk storms (so quotidian now)
so pedestrian!   drab!   so New Labour!
arriving in ties, with their Christian names
like it's the first day of school. You've got junk mail.
Does anyone else
crave some lightning from life? For their windows
to crash, just go haywire?
To find themselves lost
                        in the gossip of keys
in the whump   & the tish.

My First minipops 67 [120.2] [source field mix] *and My Second*
for and to Al

I was forced from the get-go to reclassify this music
according to my own purely pragmatic scheme of things
whereby if you can't listen to it properly while driving
above 60 k in my Dacia Logan 1.6 [16 valve upgrade]
with the incoming air set at level 2 or higher,
if too much detail, too many subtleties of the oeuvre are lost
when each tick of staccato or drawn out legato are essential,
not to mention if some hint at dissonance is erased
along with a host of pings, squelches, hissing scratches or clickety clacks,
namely all the markers [not merely among complexities
of multitudinous scapes of earthly/unearthly sound[s]]
that become coordinates revealing, by punctuating the void,
the vastness of a starry universe by playing off all the others
like birds all dotted about in the dusk of a darkening forest
held by a breezy hush or traffic passing in swishes
[which old Dacia's supply in an abundance of overkill
squashing the birds, erasing subtleties and blinding the stars];
well, I was forced to reclassify all this as classical music
and that might have been the end for Aphex Twin right there and then
if you, my most trusted music guru, hadn't been so goddam insistent.
So, into this precious hour of my Sunday afternoon
when I switch off everything bar the singular source
to have Janáček lead me backwards down some overgrown path,
I gave up my allotted hour and myself up to him instead
whereby these thump-driven swoops in rises like gusts
that scoop you up in the palms of juggling hands to a rhythm
unimposing like snapping fingers to breath-based chuckles
into which, once established, he inserts in almost ad hoc manner
a disquieting, potentially sinister new tone that has you enter
this secret garden of delights as our chuckle seems to lose
it's self-assurance while persisting in an act of self-assurance
set in an awe intensifying at times to resemble fear
in a thrilling density about the heart like the strange supportive pressures
at 12m below the surface of water that disarm laughter
which breathes on regardless, offset or set off
by new and curious wonders that press dancing all about it.
So, what I'm getting to is how *Syro* came to be stacked,
rather oddly and lonely, a slither of white and chartreuse
among the varnished woods, the brasses, long dresses, suits and bowties
on my classical rack, yet not unreasonably, don't you think so Al?

The Fizzog Technique

(Inspired by Chris Cunningham's videos for Aphex Twin)

Face it, Richard, we went face-to-face with you
because you had decided to invert your image,
to make it a totem, a dystopian vision

of opposition or just a mark of bare-faced cheek.
Face recognition, then blink, your face
in a face-off between versions of you

pasted from the ponytailed stock-image,
transfigured into the dysmorphic distortions
more commonly found stretching the limits

of gesture and taste in a Hall of Mirrors.
We find you attached to a body not your own
but still moving in time to a riptide of glitches,

a chorus of yous. It is the lock-jaw grin
we can't shrug-off, that keeps us sleepless,
facing ourselves somehow, only to interrogate

a reflection, our reveal of eyes, mouth, bone;
that imprint we keep, or show, and think we own.

Christopher Horton

Four

Got my head buried in the code again/
say *yep* when my parents call me in,
but I don't go because I'm there again/
got to hop across the bars again, enjambement
those parts and jumpstart this partition -
next: lay down that theremin
set the breakbeat off/thunder rolling in,
and get the melody in on the violin/
the counterpoint to the violence/
the lush pads down like lonely friends
and I'll remember to get the dialect in the title in
after dinner
on the fourth day
of this composition.

running commentary

nasa got a message from space today   white spirit   BC
thats funny, the walls are breathing for me   please come
to New York!!!   Having breakfast after a night with heavy
thunderstorms.   tone, texture   Memories I cant quite
remember . Moments lost in time.   Thatcher was still
prime minister   if it weren't for erotic fanfiction sites...
          Friday nights in 92/92, getting the 18.36 Thameslink from
Farringdon to Leatherhead with this on my Walkman. Beautiful.
A   P   H   E   X
hey where can i download this? plausible   sound's   warmth
Now, only a lament. Like all great fools,   You   must   know
i've always loved you   I will continue.   , delusionarily.
     I wish I could meet my old friend from hinckley back in 89.
weathered stone   I 'm on the search for the next search
There and Back Again.   please i need my blue point
          Cruising in my 100,000$ jetski in tahiti with my beautiful
wives listening to this album, my life is beautiful   The Kama
Sutra is the best Book, by the way.   NO ADS!?
     Language and communication itself have not yet developed
enough to express   my penis fell off when i listened to this
music... this is a good sign.   Shit hole fuck nuts   early
I'm drunk and adore the challenge of sidewalks.   Délicieux
love Mozart.   the dreamers of the dreams."
like polished Orb   revolving inside   la puta madre!
LISTENING TO THIS WHILE LOOKING FOR JOBS FOR JSA
AT 5AM   Where's the drop?   Periodically whenever
decay or time or any type of human measurement this includes
heat and cold   keep fluidic fluidic   listen on the bus.......
feel you are growing fro m earth ....   at least fully understand
Times just a concept   We are but a matrix of atoms
trying to make contact   YES! is   this   shit   called   "music"?
this moment slipped   dying star.   !!!! :D :D
I am the algorithm   the sound the Sun makes   already
to be alive.......   perceived   I always return to this

Hedphelym

The telephone rings but no one is there.
A rubber band abandoned by the postbox.
Butterfly wings blocks and weeks apart
Among all kinds of garbage in the streets.
Late last night I told you half my secrets.
A long assortment of empty promises,
Anonymous content in familiar voices.
Pleas to return all the proceeds fail
To convey data to the inured parties.
The watch at first ran fast now slow.
We sleep and wake all watched over
By unseen machines. A lamb invented
The wheel while wisdom slept off
Its catalog of embarrassing wonders.

meltedfamily remix ep vinyl rip 192kbps

i asked aphex twin to remix my dad

dad is a tv now, a glitch in the alcove
a 5-second loop from *match of the day* (april 1994)
static amens fritzing at the edges

i asked aphex twin to remix my mum

mum is a sculpture now, a chirping meat scribble
topiary of cheery flesh, legs and legs and legs and legs
cartwheeling like she hasn't for years

i asked aphex twin to remix my brother

now we know the answer to the question
how many pianos
can one boy become

i asked aphex twin to remix me

matringlomb jrtenpliop
conjunloninged scowrl lepagionsdts
chniynch bgognjuggetngg gmenchcklux
Inhugndeqlity mlkseris dronforkc
ha ha ha ha ha ha ha ha ha ha ha ha

Selected Ambient Works, Vol. 2, #3

then we were out
and there was me,
swaying, shell
shocked in the foxhole
of south london's
early gloom, unseen.
the saved parted company,
the pristine afterparty
called them all relentlessly;
the half light broke
the spell beneath which
i had hurt to travel.
i marvelled at their
recognition of one
another's reality,
their lust for breath,
and congenial brutality,
quickened by the press
for death, now hostile
to my lonely follow.
the silent streets lay
stretched right out
before our gaunt
and hollow faces;
the broadsheets flapping
in the wind, the hood
a garish hidden nightmare
of an echoed, absent beat,
the aching movement
of the bitter pavement,
the dumb step of our feet.
i smoked to fold
the air within,
the furtive joint
a pointless rhythm,
the cocktail held
in swirls inside,
and sighed, curbside,

to feel myself
then find myself
still rocking on
the mindless tube.
propped up on
haunches aching stoop
i watched them leaving
one by one:
an animation played,
rewound, the pound
again, an endless loop
of leonine departures,
figures that emerged
from swirls of motion
to dissolve in space,
that raced to step
across and out of me
to nothingness again.
i came lurching round
each time, to let it go,
and get out at the next stop.
but in that beam i held
inside no light intruded,
felt inside, a whispered column
of the absent question,
till without fright or fascination
i raised myself a child again.
the piccadilly storm abated,
the light an intermittent shock,
the floor still shook, an endless blow,
the hundred stamping feet below,
the throb that sought to swallow
whole - now growing slowly distant.
and in the empty space between,
a humming silence, contact
made, a fleeting sense of lethargy
inside a body marked as other.
i gathered what i had accrued,
stood statued on a well
known platform, the greater
london never home,
the sweating project
of reassurance

that I could one day be as well,
but still, for now, too gone
to stay, still shell shocked,
swaying, in the foxhole
of my head laid down
inside an empty room,
to try to sleep, to minimize
the urge to weep for having slept
the whole night through.

Aphex & Castle

The mystery of Elephant –
Faraday's cage, or was it house,
yours, hidden but glowing present
at all hours on the roundabout.
Genius below the underpass,
creating behind opaque glass?
The old boys drinking in the pub
swore they heard it in the club.
Rumour said within your bunker
(with space enough to park your tank,
and the 'Windowlicker' charabanc)
new tracks would shudder and thunder,
surfing accelerated time,
polygons waving into minds.

Drbkqs Rlmpxld (L+7)

Tracklist

CD1

1.	Qfudefaoer Fsod	2:30
2.	Coykoziu	4:58
3.	Rsakmcniuun Tijzor	2:13
4.	Vmgyjyh-Swptch14	4:59
5.	Zayoaoa Afuoe	2:19
6.	Ndeaf Teyuauz	5:15
7.	Iifkofoujooyk	2:40
8.	Jojr/Cey17	5:25
9.	Hvrpl 21st	2:12
10.	Ta Zaiua Tijoes ÷ Zaiua Tijoaesz Touua	8:17
11.	Gwhrlk9	6:53
12.	Vrbhn Lq Trx 11	1:42
13.	Auzzoiz	0:20
14.	Of a Zjbssfaz Sfm Akoanyod	2:21
15.	Rezzou Kaser	1:28

Total Length 51:54

CD2

1.	61 Jftyu Ieaaz	6:13
2.	Iaout-Youtaka	2:05
3.	Soyuakeyer	0:38
4.	XRAoy	1:34
5.	Mlltphhcl 13	6:31
6.	Bbt 11	0:32
7.	Prlp Gwhrllk 10b	1:26
8.	Maaoey	1:04
9.	Aariun Jouayos	7:21
10.	Weaiaais Je Oakui	2:18
11.	Yunseu Oosou	1:56
12.	Hfx244 v.14	4:30
13.	Zpggvmhtpc 24	8:42
14.	Blskhb10lpnm	2:17
15.	Nhnvb9	3:32

Total Length 49.01

Your call is important to us

Thank you for contacting Aphex Twin customer support
Your call may be monitored and sent to a server
Buried under five-thousand feet of blue earth
For quality purposes
To continue in English press 1
For Binary press 0

All our agents are currently
Dressed as big pink bears
With enormous heads
Please hold
A representative will be with you shortly
There are 85-92 people ahead of you in the queue

If your enquiry is about synthetic moon dust press #
If you're calling not for an answer but a mood press play
We apologise for the delay lay ay
We regret the rreevveerrbb
We lament the low pass filter
We deplore the distortion

We bemoan nothing
And you are nothing
But a purple handstand
A parboiled hatband
Curtailed headland
Curdled strand

Thank you for contacting Aphex Twin customer support
My name is Gwely Mernans
Do you ever get the feeling
Your life is like one long queue
For a flight you've already missed
To the destination of someone else's dreams?

Contributors

Sophie Taylor

Sophie Taylor is a visual artist from Newcastle, who pursued a career in writing after studying Film and Sound Design at the Royal College of Art. Her texts have been published via Permeable Barrier, Pamenar Press, LUVA, Lychee Zine and Spun Press amongst others, with a poetry collection launched via The NewBridge Project last year. Moonlighting as a late night radio show host and creating dialogue for AI characters, her work moves between audio, verse and script.

Katie Oliver

Katie Oliver has been shortlisted for the Bridport Prize, the Bath Flash Award and most recently the Short Fiction/University of Essex Wild Writing Prize. She has further work published in various places including Lunate Fiction, Molotov Cocktail, X-R-A-Y and Dust Poetry, and is a first reader for Forge Literary Magazine and Tiny Molecules. She can be found on Twitter @katie_rose_o

Fiona Glen

Fiona Glen is an emerging writer from Edinburgh, based in London. Bridging essay, poetry, script, and fiction, her texts explore messy embodiment, unruly ecologies, and how human beings understand themselves through objects and other species. Glen graduated in 2020 from the MA Writing at the Royal College of Art, with the manuscript for a book that follows the slippery figure of the octopus through contemporary culture. She has read her work at various London venues including the Science Museum, and she has previously been commissioned by BBC x ICA New Creatives.

Naomi Marklew

Naomi Marklew is based in Durham in the North of England. Her writing can be found online and in print in *-algia, streetcake, Selcouth Station, Untitled:Voices* and *The Aesthetic Directory*, amongst other places. She has a PhD in contemporary poetry and her work features in the film *Growing Home* commissioned for the 2021 Durham Book Festival. She tweets @ NaomiMarklew and her website is https://naomimarklew.wixsite.com/ website.

Jared Schwartz

Jared Schwartz is a writer from New York and a student at Brown University. His work has been published or is forthcoming in Glassworks Magazine, North Dakota Quarterly, FEED, Eunoia Review, and Anthropocene. In addition to writing, he plays the bass guitar and occasionally records music. He can be found on Instagram and Twitter @jschwartzpoetry.

Dan Power

Dan Power is a poet living in Dundee. His first pamphlet, *PREDICTIVE TEXT POEMS*, was published by Spam Press in 2016, and *more like this* was published by If A Leaf Falls Press in 2020. The pamphlet *late morning* (Legitimate Snack) and graphic novel *SELECTED DREAMS* (Steel Incisors) are forthcoming. Dan is the founding editor of Trickhouse Press, which he hopes you'll check out at trickhousepress.com | He/him, @ therealdanpower

Kenneth M Cale

Kenneth M Cale lives in Oregon and is the author of two chapbooks, *Midnight Double Feature* (Sweat Drenched Press) and *elsewhen* (Ghost City Press), both published in 2020. Recent work can be found in *Beir Bua Journal* and *Petrichor* as well as in the anthology *The Mouth of a Lion* (Steel Incisors, 2021). You can also find him on Twitter: @kmcale81

Maria Sledmere

Maria Sledmere is an artist, poet, member of A+E Collective and editor-in-chief at SPAM Press. Her debut collection, The Luna Erratum, is out now from Dostoyevsky Wannabe.

Wesley Finch

Wesley Finch is a Midlands based musician and writer who also works with various arts and charity organisations in his local area. Twitter: @wesfinch

Barney Ashton-Bullock

Barney Ashton-Bullock is a music researcher and project manages album re-issues for the SFE Record Label at Cherry Red and for London Records. He is a published poet; 'Mottled Memoirs' (2014, Cherry Red), 'Schema/ Stasis' (2017, Society Club Press), 'Cafe Kaput!' (2020, Broken Sleep Books), F**kpig Zeitgeist! (2021, Cherry Red) & 'Bucolicism - Alt-lite lyric verse for a post-pastoral England' (2021, Cherry Red). He is the poet in the Downes Braide Association prog-pop band and songwriter / dramaturg for the 'Andy Bell is Torsten' poetry, music and theatre collective starring Erasure's Andy Bell.

Charlie Baylis

Charlie Baylis is from Nottingham. He is the Editor of Anthropocene and the Chief Editorial Advisor of Broken Sleep Books. His poetry has been nominated twice for the Pushcart Prize and once for the Forward Prize, he has also been shortlisted for a Saboteur Award for Best Reviewer of Literature. His most recent publication is *Santa Lucía* (Invisible Hand Press). He spends his spare time completely adrift of reality.

Jack Stacey

Jack Stacey is a Creative Writing BA and MA graduate from the University of Winchester. He's had poems featured in New River Press, Anthropocene Poetry and Vaine Magazine. He has also directed a play for the Theatre Royal in Winchester, and is currently attempting to write, as well as act, in plays and tv shows.

Trent Oven

Trent Oven lives in Ipswich, where he works in anger management. This is his first poem.

CD Boyland

CD Boyland (@chrisdboyland) is a [d]eaf poet who lives in Cumbernauld near Glasgow, Scotland. Debut pamphlet 'User Stories', published by Stewed Rhubarb Press. Other visual/experimental work published by or forthcoming in 3AM Magazine, Aww-Struck (PoemAtlas online exhibition), Beia Bua Journal and elsewhere.

Calum Rodger

Calum Rodger is a Glasgow-based poet working in print, performance and digital forms. His publications include Occasional Poems 2012-2019 (Speculative Books, 2020), PORTS (SPAM Press, 2019) and Know Yr Stuff: Poems on Hedonism (Tapsalteerie, 2014).

Adam Heardman

Adam Heardman is a poet and writer from Newcastle upon Tyne. His poems have appeared in *PN Review*, *PAIN*, *Belleville Park Pages*, *eyot*, and more. He lives and works in East London.

Anna Kirwin

Anna Kirwin is a writer and artist, living in London, but dreaming of the Arctic. Her last published piece considered exploration, but more generally, her recent work deals with language, thought and time. She sees light in the darkness.

Alastair Hesp

A poet from Yorkshire, England but who fled from Tory Britain over 10 years ago. Currently studying an MA at The Manchester Writing School (from distance). His poetry has appeared in anthologies and journals such as *The Verve Press Anthologies*, *Acid Bath Publishing Anthology* and *The French Literary Review*. Asides from formal publications, he explores interdisciplinary work in live/improvised performances with musician Tatu Rönkkö, a poetic art installation and a sequence poem for a dance performance in Copenhagen. It was in an underground Berlin club Alastair claims he stood next to AFX as they both watched a legendary techno pioneer and record label producer who happens to be a distant relative of Otto von Bismarck. He still stubbornly stands by this story today.

Dan Melling

Dan Melling is a writer from Skegness. His work has appeared in The Rialto, Fanzine, Juked and elsewhere. He sometimes tweets at @melling_dan.

Karina Bush

Karina is an Irish writer and artist who lives in Rome. Her work has been published by Tangerine Press, Akashic Books, Expat Press, Ragged Lion Press, the International Poetry Studies Institute, The Nervous Breakdown, and more. In summer 2021, Tangerine Press published her fourth book 'Rotten Milk', which is a signed limited-edition collection of poetry. For more visit karinabush.com or follow her on Instagram @karinabushxx

Joshua Blackman

Joshua Blackman is a poet, writer and photographer who lives in Chichester, UK. His poems have appeared in Ambit, the White Review, Moth Magazine and various other publications. joshuablackman.co.uk

Paul Ings

Born in Bournemouth UK 1971, now 29 years in the Czech Republic working as teacher and translator. Poetry published in magazines including The Reader, Magma, The Interpreter's House, Ink Sweat and Tears, Salzburg Poetry review, South, etc., and anthologies: *Hildegard* (Poetry on the Lake), *Eternal* (Hammond House) and *Cornwall* (Palores Publications). Joint winning poem in Exmoor Society poetry competition 2019, translations of Czech poetry (BODY Literature), (Poetry Cornwall) and reviews in Czech journal Plav.

Christopher Horton

Christopher Horton's poems have appeared in Poetry London, Poetry Wales, Ambit, Magma and anthologies with Penned in the Margins, tall-lighthouse and Days of Roses. He has been a prize-winner in the National Poetry Competition, the South Downs Poetry Festival Poetry Prize and the Bridport Prize. His first pamphlet is published by tall-lighthouse.

Ben Armstrong

Ben Armstrong is a poet and editor from the Black Country, UK and an alumnus of the Warwick Writing Programme. His first collection, *Perennial*, was published by Knives, Forks and Spoons Press in 2019.

Esme Huānhuān

Esme was born, abandoned and found in Nanfeng. She now lives, works and writes in London. Her poetry appears in Sinθ, amberflora and SOFT, amongst others.

Aaron Fagan

Aaron Fagan was born in Rochester, New York, in 1973 and is the author of *Garage* (Salt Publishing, 2007), *Echo Train* (Salt Publishing, 2010), and *A Better Place Is Hard to Find* (The Song Cave, 2020).

Stefan Mohamed

Stefan Mohamed is a performing poet, author and freelance editor based in Bristol. He is the author of poetry pamphlet *The Marketplace of Ideas* (Stewed Rhubarb), spoken word collection *PANIC!* (Burning Eye Books) and novels *The Bitter Sixteen Trilogy* and *Falling Leaves* (Salt Publishing). His poetry and comedy videos can be found at youtube.com/bigdumbvoid, and he is always on Twitter (@stefmowords) and occasionally on Facebook (StefMoWriter).

Robert Bal

Robert Bal is a poet of the south Asian diaspora and is currently a visitor on Squamish, Musqueam and Tsleil-waututh First Nations land in North America. His poetry often explores growing up a male-coded person of colour in London, England, in the aftermath of the colonial experience and the age of late stage capitalism.

James Davies

James Davies' latest books are the minimalist sequence *Forty-Four Poems and a Volta* and the short story *The Ten Superstrata of Stockport J. Middleton* – a translation of the first page of Philip K. Dick's *The Three Stigmata of Palmer Eldritch*. Currently the editor of if p then q, he also edited Matchbox and co-organised The Other Room reading series. His book-length poem *stack* is a list of minimalist walking performances. Find out more at www.jamesdaviespoetry.com

Ben Blench

Ben Blench is a freelance copywriter who writes poems and songs to escape from the day job. He has translated two books, *Why I Love Tattoos* and *Why I Love Sex*, and still regrets the time he had to turn down an assignment to write a manifesto for biscuits. He lives in Amsterdam.

L950ay16outy10 [163.97][ourun rest mix]

www.ingramcontent.com/pod-product-compliance
Lightning Source LLC
Chambersburg PA
CBHW021942040426
42448CB00008B/1196